The Difference Between a Manager and a Leader

Jimmy Dillard

Contents

Dedication

All leaders that I have had. In some way you have helped me professionally.

Acknowledgments

Special thanks to all that have been a key part of this! Thank you all for viewing and inspiring me to continue with this project.

Introduction

Loving	**L**eave	**L**oving	**L**ead
Every	**E**verything	**E**mpathetic	**E**qually
Aspect	**A**ccessible	**A**dmirable	**A**micably
Delicately	**D**istinguished	**D**ynamic	**D**iversified

Each of the aforementioned is a version of leading in a quality manner. Often, we accept the individual above us based on each organization's structure. Each team member has an opinion but will abide by what the organization wants.

Now, how do we fix this, you ask?

Well, it's easier than you think! It's quality training.

When I began my career in management, I didn't know what I was supposed to do other than meet the standard goals metric-wise, smile at people, or even walk around. They outlined what good numbers looked like; they outlined the customer complaints and how to respond to them by offering a financial element. Not once did they teach me how to LEAD my team.

I had a mentor who met me and couldn't believe my story. He told me that **no money or no award could beat the fact that I was where I**

was at that day! At that moment, I had no idea what he really was saying till 5 years later. He would be tough on me as I went about my days, weeks, months, and years. He often used to tell me I was better than the people I reported to and that I could run that organization one day.

On one hand, I would laugh and think he was crazy. But on the other hand, I felt that I became one of the best because of him. When he started with me, it was about knowledge and understanding. He took the time to give me opportunities to fix problems and fail. Again, not once did I see what the bigger picture was. After several failed attempts, he explained what I saw, understood, and proceeded.

Fast forward 12 years, and now I look back, and he didn't manage me. **He LED me**.

Part 1: Management vs. Leadership: Exploring the Subtleties

What does it mean to be a "**MANAGER**"?

Let's look at the root word "manage" and what it means:

"To handle or direct with a degree of skill." or "To exercise executive, administrative, and supervisory direction."

Now, most times, that is what the average person says they do in their day or what they were told they were supposed to do. In all fairness, sometimes senior management (notice I didn't refer to the term senior leadership) views this as the goal. And that's okay for them. But is it okay for the frontline workforce? **No**.

Our frontline workforce often views the manager and what they do and say as the right way. No fault to them, considering that's what they have grown to know. It's a standard in a lot of industries as well as a lot of corporations. But how do we invoke the change? It starts with **QUALITY TRAINING**.

Now, what does it mean to be a leader? Let's look at the root word "**lead**":

"To guide on a way especially by going in advance" or "To direct on a course or in a direction."

How many of us can say that we have felt those 2 examples fit our everyday lives? Not many! Leadership is built, not bought. It's a trait that many people possess; however, some do not have it from the start. This, in that case, has to be instilled. This quote I once heard from one of my previous Leaders stuck with me:

> *"The bottom line in leadership isn't how far we advance ourselves but how far we advance others."*

That is impactful for many reasons, but I will point out that this has been very fortifying for me because when I see this from some professionals I have led, it means the world to me!

The Rise

"We would like to extend an offer to you. This position will start next Monday. Your manager will meet you and do some training with you".

This is how it starts. You hear the start date and the word "**training**." But let's make sense of what "training" truly is.

Every industry is different, but we are told that we will receive training from a manager at some point. The level of training, the duration of the training, and the curriculum are all unknown. I have seen many managers hired "trained" by their managers; however, the training consists of learning how to make rules on their emails, walk and observe, or even ensure the company gives you everything it has to offer.

What's missing? **How to lead your team**.

Essentially, everyone hired as a manager has the traits or qualities of a leader. But if the focus isn't on those attributes, it is easy to forget that you possess them. One of the first moves I recommended is remembering a great leader you once had, and what you considered a bad leader you also may have had. This is essential because you emulate most of what the good leader possesses.

From a poor leader, you learn what **not** to do. Discerning good and bad practices is crucial as you begin leading your new team. Navigating through the organization will be challenging, but remember, every ocean has unique waves, yet they are all parts of the same vast sea.

Next, getting to know the team is integral to getting off to a good start. Many teams want to have a great leader. They often can tell you all about the previous leaders (good and bad) and, based on that, a subtle hint to you of their expectations.

The best advice in this situation is to be yourself. You are where you are for a reason. You already took a huge step if you think about it. You listened to what they had to say. Most employees just want to be heard. Another big item for employees is follow-up. If you don't have an answer right away, let them know that you will reach out to the proper department and follow up, but please make sure you follow up. It is critical to remember that because you never want to give misinformation. This could cause your team to lose confidence or distrust you.

Now, how do you continue this positive trend?

First, pride yourself in knowing what the team knows. I recommend you be able to do the work you ask of them. As that is a focus, you should always know the procedure but also know why the procedure is in place. This will give your team a sense of security.

Challenge yourself to attend the training to become a subject matter expert. Although this is a humbling task, it will garner the respect you receive from your team. This is huge for all leaders! Humility is difficult; however, it is a trait that all leaders have learned to accept, which is 1 of the biggest reasons they are considered a leader and not a manager.

Again, the team will see this and follow. They will respect your words, your actions, and most importantly...YOU! This is all you truly want from them. They respect you, and everything else will follow. How do you maintain the respect is the key. Be fair, consistent, available, and open to difficult conversations. Sometimes, consistency is challenging based on each scenario or day. The biggest advice I can give you is that employees see that in most companies, **the biggest consistency is 'inconsistency.'**

Addressing that and correcting that 1 opportunity at a time is key. There will be some people who aren't all up for it; however, being treated fairly regardless of who they are or their tenure will bring the optics to reality. Remember this quote from Benjamin Franklin as you get to this point:

> *"Tell me, and I forget. Teach me, and I remember. Involve me, and I learn."*

Let's look at this from a Birds Eye. When you look at your current superior, what makes them a leader, or are they a manager? What have they done to separate the two?

Let's say you see them as a leader. According to the previously mentioned, they demonstrate a "developing" level to give them this title. How do you accept the direction they give you? How do you perform the task they have assigned you? Do you question what they have assigned you? Or do you do it based on how you see them as leader? These questions run through my mind when there is a question of which category fits the individual.

Now, let's say you see them as a manager. When they assign a task, what is your first thought? Do you question how this is even part of your job? When they deliver some news, do you question the validity of it? How about when they arrive after you? However, they are gone before you can address an issue you may have encountered. Which style (leader or manager) are you more likely to emulate?

A manager once told me she comes to work so her team won't ask her questions. A leader once told me, "Every day, you build your team by being available and knowledgeable."

The irony is that this is the same individual who, at one point in her career, worked for a manager and, at the latter point, a leader.

Honestly, many great leaders face this situation. The common factor is their ability to recognize the difference and prioritize it for both themselves and their teams. Are there professionals who only go as far as managers in their careers? Absolutely! Some become senior managers or Vice Presidents of a department or company, which, in their eyes, is the prize. If you speak to the employees that report to them, you often see/hear of the bad morale or notice that the attrition is extremely high, not due to them finding higher paying jobs or better jobs, but they do not like the company's leadership.

"People don't quit jobs; they quit managers."

Often, there isn't a direct correlation because we don't strive to give what we receive if we are managers. This is why when we get great leaders, we have a blueprint to follow. This is the standard we want to make as a focus.

Here is a thought: how do you give 110% daily? Naturally, it's by going above and beyond. But what does that look like? In a world with countless industries, achieving 110% means being accessible, welcoming questions, valuing feedback, and genuinely caring for every team member, regardless of their tenure or title. That's the hallmark of a true leader. They give the extra 10%, and it's organic. You don't have to try to be what you aren't. No one should say that you are "trying." You were trying when no one was looking so that it's on full display when everyone is looking. This is where you start to notice that your team follows your lead. They always want to do the right thing. They can tell you many reasons; however, they see you! Orrin Woodward has this quote that I used to write on a sticky when I felt that I wasn't "leading" according to my principles. It made me realize that I was. I just saw a flaw or missed a minor detail that made me feel or see something wrong, but I still was leading. He said:

"Average leaders raise the bar on themselves; good leaders raise the bar for others; great leaders inspire others to raise their own bar."

I would read this, and it reminds me that leaders influence, guide, teach, and set an example. Your success as a leader will come from different angles. The constant will be that you have created and set a precedent for yourself and your team. As they follow, you will continue to strive to be a better leader. They will not allow you to stop. Your drive will drive them. Your focus will help them focus. Your passion will build their passion. Always remember not everyone can be a leader. Those who become that must continue to improve and build on every positive and negative. Adversity will come, and this is where you, as a leader, will thrive. Continue to display to the managers around you. They will be looking, believe me. No matter what, remember that your team is the priority!

The Balancing Act

One of the hardest challenges in becoming a leader is balancing motivation and discipline. The problem is that you haven't figured out the difference until you become a leader. The biggest questions are how/when to use the correct tool or whether it is warranted. You will have help to a degree. Your senior leader will guide you on more pressing or higher-level issues requiring certain disciplinary actions. That will help; however, what happens when you face a challenging decision you must address?

A manager more than likely will make it easy for themselves. It's easy for them because it's simple: the employee made a mistake, so here is the discipline: they will tell them to sign it and accept it point blank–a short conversation, no coaching involved, or if it was coaching involved, it was simple probably something like this "don't do it again." It's a very easy process for them because they are "exercising executive, administrative, and supervisory direction." Just in case we forgot what it meant to manage. How does this benefit the employee? Well, I can think of only 1 reason: they don't have to deal with this manager in a long sitting–very disappointing for a corporation and from an employee's point of view.

Now, let's look at the opposite, a leader. First, if a senior leader sends them directions for a higher-level action that warrants strict discipline, they will make sure they understand what happened, what rule was broken, and why this is the level of discipline being issued. This is natural because leaders want to be in sync with their team as much as possible. Giving them the 5 W's (who, what, when, where, why) is the key to success.

I will admit that it's sometimes challenging or intimidating to issue discipline. It's even sometimes hard based on how great an employee they are. It's something we must do to keep the integrity of our workplace leveled. When discussing, you must remember that your approach drives the behavior and the employee's understanding. Your leadership and professionalism will be what they see and drive the conversation to an understanding for them. Reminding them of the value they bring to the team is critical! Everyone plays a part in the success of the company. The feeling of them being valued, as well as how important their role is to the organization, can also ease the conversation.

Not all of your team will accept the disciplinary conversations the same. And that's okay. As a leader, you must understand that you have to learn to speak to each audience. Now, is this easy? **No**. But you should know your team and understand what drives and motivates them, which can help.

I once had the privilege of working for an amazing lady who used to tell me every time she comes into town, I need to give her at least 1 fun fact about a different team member. Initially, I shook my head (not physically because she would've seen it), thinking it was a waste of my time. I then thought if I didn't, she would not show me the amazing side anymore, so I better. Guess what.... I loved it! It helped me see that I could relate to each of the team members and allowed me to speak to each of them (all together) at every town hall or quarterly meeting.

Discipline is defined as:

"The quality of being able to behave and work in a controlled way which involves obeying particular rules or standards"

The best approach is up to you. I recommend allowing the employee to explain what's being addressed, outline the procedural reference, and ask if they understood it. This gives the employee an understanding, gives them the company's view of what happened, and provides coaching (this does wonders. It allows you and the employee to agree and makes it easier if a next-level discipline must be issued). As I'm coaching, I give scenarios where the understanding is proven. This gives you the proof that you discussed, you've coached, and lastly, you allowed the employee to understand from the company's view.

Another indicator that this will be effective is ensuring they understand they are essential to your company's success. When you have a tougher situation to meet about, always remember to communicate without anger, always speak professionally, and never forget that you are to support. Just because it's a disciplinary meeting doesn't mean you lose your servant-leader skills. This is when they should be on display at the highest point.

It's hard to do the discipline when you are non-confrontational. To make matters worse, sometimes you don't agree. But you must ensure that your consistency and integrity as a leader aren't questioned. Although it's you and the employees meeting, other employees will watch, assume, and even makeup stories about how so and so got away with it. And that's okay because you will be a LEADER in this situation and do what's expected of you. If there is doubt, you will take it out of the air and prove you are where you are at for a reason!

Reaching the Meaning

I often say that I was given an opportunity to manage but realized that the team that reported to me was better than what they accepted. When I took this title, I had an idea of what I needed to do. To be clear,

I'm going to yell it out loud so it remains in my daily life. I'VE NEVER FORGOTTEN WHERE I CAME FROM!

This is often the biggest reason managers do not become leaders. They forget. We have all had opportunities to see and think about what we want to change in a company, but how many of us continue navigating through the ranks to affect it? All of us because leaders should be doing just that. Anyone who started this as a manager is no longer a manager! This is where you understood, took the final leap, and became a LEADER! We have seen the value of a leader, we have seen the harsh reality of a manager, and we have heard how to be what our teams need. Now, let's break it down so that it's not forgotten.

Leading is a privilege. Your team allows you to make a difference in their lives, help them grow, and guide them so that they reach the success that the company needs and their personal success. I'm going to return to a quote:

"Average leaders raise the bar on themselves; good leaders raise the bar for others; great leaders inspire others to raise their own bar."

This will be your goal! This is so powerful because the quote is what it is all about. Your team has shown you this. They are following the leader. Sometimes, you are drained or tired, but because you are a great leader, your team has raised the bar on themselves and picked you up! How amazing would that feel? Let's say that each team member comes and gives you 5 minutes of their day and tells you daily how they will achieve success. What does that tell you? That you are leading this team! I've been a part of a team led by a wonderful lady who would challenge us to the degree that we wanted to prove to her that we could do anything she could put in front of us. No matter how challenging, we would find a way to achieve it. As I looked back years later, I always wanted her to be proud of us and know we were here when she wasn't herself.

Your team has seen the good, the bad, and the ugly. They know the leader they have will do whatever it takes for them. Do you know your team? Do you see the strides that your team has made? Do you have a rapport with each of them? Do you relate to each of them in one way or another? These are all questions that, when we started, the answer probably was no.

At this point, if it's still no since people are your purpose, let's start focusing, so the answer to those questions is yes! Does it mean you aren't a good leader? Absolutely not! This means you are working hard to be what they deserve and want. They still respect you. They still follow you. They are still more engaged than before. You're on the right path and will reach where you need to be. Through everything, the leader gives everyone a sense of certainty and is well worth every hill climbed.

I want you to remember this: great leaders have these 2 traits no matter what obstacle they face: empathy and perspective. It's not about being in charge; it's about taking care of those under our charge. This gives all that follows you the vision and the smile at the end. Nothing is just good enough anymore. The standard is set, and it's the minimum your team and you will be. Don't look back. Your team does that for you. They won't look ahead because they are following the leader they chose to trust to follow. Lastly, you have given others the vision that they can become a leader. They will see you and tell others about you. Each title brings a higher level of leadership. You will grow with that title. The expectation will be a lot more on paper, but the core values you have gained through all of this. Plug and play what you are missing as the titles change. There is always room for more. Remember.... you are a LEADER! Only you can take that away from you.

Part 2: Tackling the Unconscious Bias

The mind thinks as fast as you read, write, talk, and listen. These are standard senses that are traditional to the average human being. One way that this is proven is through what we call the Unconscious Bias. For those who never heard this, let's break this down for you. Unconscious bias is a stereotype or prejudice that we hold against groups of people without the individual consciously knowing we are doing it. There are many types of unconscious biases. To name a few: affinity, ageism, beauty, confirmation, gender, and conformity. These biases are very common to leaders who are new or even experienced. I like to think that we can fix this by mentally understanding that we all have a significance to being coworkers and no one is better than the next. We can tackle this by understanding the biases and how to avoid them.

Affinity bias is when you like someone or tend to connect with someone based on similar experiences, backgrounds, or interests. A good example is when your company hires individuals based on a "**cultural fit**." This is not necessarily helping your corporation grow or even add diversity. This is potentially can hinder them. As a leader, we must be cautious of the notion that "they have to be like me," or better yet, make sure you can understand the difference between skills and attributes so that you aren't adding them to your team based on the Affinity Bias.

Ageism Bias is maybe one of the hardest to avoid. This is when you have a negative feeling or thought towards another individual based on age. To be fair, it can go against the younger age group, but it affects the older age group more often. It tends to hurt the older work groups because many believe the narrative that "**as you age, changing careers is challenging**," but the reality is that leaders value the younger generation. I have always told many new leaders that experience is taught over time. There isn't an overnight expert. Or even "**an expert in something was once a beginner**." Avoiding this bias is simple: NO DISCRIMINATION! No matter the age, each employee adds value to the corporation. Diversity should be a part of our consciousness regardless of age.

Beauty Bias is one of the more common. This biased behavior suggests attractive people are more competent, qualified, and successful. This is a social behavior. Does beauty make you more intelligent? No, it does not. This bias has been addressed with many layers of scrutiny for several years. We must remember that your looks aren't what separates you from the next individual. Your work ethic, knowledge, and principles are a few that do that. We fix this bias by allowing ourselves as leaders to treat each team member equally regardless of looks and using the structured training that your corporation has provided.

Confirmation Bias blocks your unbiased merit. Since it's blocked, it allows you to decide based on beliefs or personal desires. The best examples are someone's name, the geographical location where they grew up, or even what college they attended. This bias is simple:

limiting personalization and making a standard way of evaluating each team member. This levels the playing field for each team member and allows everyone the opportunity to stand out.

Gender Bias is preferencing one gender over another. This is a tendency of many leaders based in the industry. I once worked with a manager who told me that since one gender is overpopulating the other, let's even the ranks. I advised that, at this point, it should be over to the best candidate for the role. Naturally, it's a tough call to change the minds of individuals who know what is in front of them or what history has taught them. I often teach leaders that diversity should be prominent, allowing the company to be held accountable.

Conformity Bias is also known as "peer pressure." This is self-explanatory; however, as a leader, you want to ensure you are not asking anyone to be who they aren't. More so, you don't want your team to feel the need to act like you, which isn't their personal belief. To fix this bias, I have often found that complimenting a belief or a thought they may have shared with you will allow them to be themselves. None of us should look at someone and think they aren't like me, so they aren't okay. Please make sure we allow each team member to display themselves proudly.

The unconscious bias impacts everyone professionally. The impact can be employee development, performance reviews, and delegation of duties. Once again, this is also can be a form of DISCRIMINATION! Your team can start to suspect, leading to low morale, mistrust, and losing potential great and talented team members. All this is because we act on a bias. How do we combat this behavior? How do you assure your team that you are affording everyone equal opportunity? You do this by giving what you were trying to sell to them at one point. They need to see diversity amongst the ranks. They need to be given the same respect regardless of gender. They must be allowed to display their just as talented as the next team member. These are ways to beat the narratives and impact your team so they continue to want to improve.

Managing UP

Often, a corporation will send out a yearly survey regarding how the company is doing or what the company can do better. I've always wondered how honest people are on those surveys. To be honest, this could be a positive yearly if everyone took the opportunity throughout the year to give feedback to our leaders. Now, this is difficult for some because they fear retaliation. Well, every great leader wants feedback so that they can improve. This is also what we call "Managing UP". Now, what does this exactly mean? This means that your leader should accept the feedback, and you should be able to see the impact of the feedback one way or another, lest you take a deeper dive into this.

This is important because managing is a two-way street. If you drive results and give quality effort, you should be rewarded. Sometimes, those efforts aren't noticed. It could be challenging; however, this is where your feedback (managing up) comes into play. They should notice what you do even when it's minimal. If your effort is on the low end, or there are multiple complaints about you, do you feel they will notice that? YES!!! They will notice it, and there will be a conversation.

This is why it is okay to hold them accountable as well. Let's look at ways to manage up effectively:

Expectations! From the beginning, there needs to be expectations coming from both sides. For example, effective communication. How can I meet this deadline if I don't have the full details? How can I complete this task without guidance since this is my first time seeing these items?

Work culture is a huge one. Although you will continue to do what's asked of you, it still should be a priority as your team will feel this. I often tell my team that we are a family. If you truly think about it, depending on your total working hours and commute, you see your coworkers more than your family on most days. The culture should reflect this. Setting this as a priority for your team by making sure you use this to manage up will give your team a positive outlook.

You want your leader to hold you and themselves accountable. Again, this goes hand in with the expectations, but the difference is accountability comes in many forms. I once advised my leader that I could tell they didn't know how to lead me since all my reviews had nothing but positives. Considering I had forgotten a deadline, I should've been held accountable. However, I did hold them accountable because I disagreed with my review due to my errors, resulting in them looking at me as if I was wrong. My review was corrected, and it started her improving as a leader.

No Micromanaging

Now, this is difficult for some. However, you must open up about this as soon as it begins. If your leader is going to delegate, they should empower you to champion the task they have delegated to you. I read a quote online that every leader should consider once they are promoted to the next level:

"The best leaders have fired themselves from their previous jobs."

This impacts you because your leader, who once used to do your role, is no longer doing it. They can advise or guide you, but they shouldn't tell you how to do it the way they do it because they have moved on from it. This is tough for many leaders because of their success at the previous level. But it's a point of emphasis of managing up.

Being Forthcoming

Now, naturally, you would believe that your leader would be honest, tell you the truth, and do it with as much advance notice as possible. Does it happen like that? Well, that's part of you managing up. I just advise a leader that I know that they should be honest and upfront with everything. Some items might upset your team, but I promise they will appreciate your honesty. This conversation is one of the easiest, considering your leader needs you to drive results. You should automatically jump to this in one of your first sit-downs.

Part 3: Leading with a vision

As a leader, you will see the good, the bad, and the ugly. There will be ups and downs. There will be moments when you realize why you are a leader and moments at the beginning where you question your ability to lead. The first message is if you are going to be a 9-5 leader, that's where and why you will question your ability. Great leaders are also 5-9 leaders. Now, what does that mean? Simple, you are available to your team when they need you. The 5-9 didn't specify am or pm. Does that mean you need to be physically at work? No. It could be a phone call, a text, or even an email. Every leader will have certain team members who require more than others. Everyone on your team is unique in their own way, which is why your team is special to you. Some will require them to call you <u>at 8 pm on Friday</u> to tell you about a problem they had. Some won't even talk to you till they see you. The constant is you are available to them.

Now, we have had some changes to our workforce over the last 4 years. We have gone through a pandemic that halted many industries and well-made labor cheaper at the height of the pandemic. As a leader, your biggest question is simple: pre-Covid or post-Covid?

Let's go pre-Covid. Leading at this time was essentially based on a tough standard from the Sr. Management of your company. The demand was higher, meaning being okay wasn't good enough. Oftentimes, you would have to coach your team based on an unreal standard; however, more often than not, the goal was achieved. As I look back at my experience, a lot was unspoken because your workforce was more senior; they worked together for quite some time and grew to accept the challenges you set forth for them. It was the "family" feeling I referenced earlier. To be fair, there were still challenging times leading at this point, but the 1 constant is that more of your team knew their purpose on the team and made sure the others did as well. Post-COVID brought a different animal. I often tell many leaders that this brought the narrative that many corporations learned to do more with/for less.

In full transparency, it was almost natural because there wasn't much going on as families were reuniting, industries were seeking financial assistance, and the more a company attempted to do, it would backfire due to the spread of the virus. Through all of that, the economy suffered, and there were safety measures in place to ensure that we could attempt to go back to our normal.

Well, we learned a new normal. A good example is restaurants and liquor. Pre-Covid, you couldn't take an alcoholic beverage outside of the restaurant. Post-COVID, they were making full menus, including alcohol to go. A good example is aviation experience, which was almost mandatory pre-Covid to be hired. As for post-Covid, training was available. There was no problem with hiring and no experience post-Covid if training was going to be adequate.

Let's be honest...the training was not at all. The standard was lowered. We did ZOOM or TEAMS training sessions, which financially benefited the corporations but hurt the workforce. Leading the post-Covid team brought many challenges. I think many leaders will agree with this, but a lot was missing from the training. Leaders had to become trainers to equate the missing element of in-person training. I think this also separated leaders from managers.

To this day, we, as leaders, still face these challenges. Will it get better? I want to say yes. We learn monthly, quarter over quarter, and year over year. As a leader, I have challenged every level of my team to be better and set a new standard. This is what you should do. We are still doing more with less; however, the old question of 'quality or quantity' is right before us. Achieve both! Use your leadership skills, grow your team, and empower every leader under you. One quick and easy way is to get your pre-Covid details, compare them to post-Covid, and see how and where you can improve. Build your team daily to get the same quality that brought the quantity pre-Covid.

Empowerment

The definition of empowerment is:

"granting of power, right, or authority to perform various acts or duties."

How do leaders fair with this aspect? How well do we do this? There is a trick to empowerment. It's called not micromanaging. Previously, we discussed not micromanaging and how it could affect your team. Well, let's empower your team. There are many ways to empower your team. 1. trust and delegation. Simple, give the tools needed as well as an authority without Interfering. 2. effective listening and communication. This will establish your expectations as well as provide guidance. This also allows for your team member to give their suggestions or concerns. 3. develop and support. This will enable them to learn new skills, advance their knowledge in areas of weakness, and unlock their full potential.

I tend to ask for volunteers to lead certain projects. Sometimes, I delegate based on strengths and weaknesses. Occasionally, we begin together, and once the plan starts coming together, I empower my team to complete it as desired. There shouldn't be any regrets, considering you have led and shown the way for your team. You have given them all the necessary tools to produce the desired results. Another strategy is empowering them to decide without consulting you in your absence. This is another big challenge for leaders, especially those with the FOMO (Fear of Missing out). Let me tell you, you will know one way or another. It's either going to be good, or it could be a horrible one. Either way, it's coming back to you.

Leader Unlocked and Achieved

It's not a sprint. It's a marathon. The results might seem like it's happening in a week or two, but you want long-term consistency. You can have short-term goals; however, the long-term effect is what you wish to last. Each leader takes the opportunity to see the goal and go for it. You can't be that without your team. You will always be as good as your team is. You have learned many ways to make your team great while becoming a great leader. Always stay focused, and the goals will be achievable. Always give your team guidance and leadership, and success will follow. Always keep the course. Even when it seems like it's all for nothing, be the leader who gives your team hope. When the impossible is expected of you, tackle it by showing your team that no task is too tall. Be the servant leader that gives your team twice as much as they give you. Lead them by example. Provide the necessary feedback.

Discipline as needed. Stay firm and consistent. Don't turn your eye to those whose unconscious bias causes problems for your team. Tackle the unconscious bias!! Manage up! The accountability to your leader will give your team confidence and support. Allow your team to manage with you! Know your audience. Be able to provide the same feedback to each member of your team. Lead all team members equally whether they have 10 years, 5 years, or 3 months. Everyone is equal. Empower your team. Give them the push they may need, but allow them to do it in your absence. Allow them to make decisions, and you respect them. Lastly, LEAD! It's what you choose, and you are who your leader has chosen.

www.ingramcontent.com/pod-product-compliance
Lightning Source LLC
Chambersburg PA
CBHW060020300526
45794CB00003B/1226